Sticker French for School

Written by Amanda Doyle
Illustrated by Ian Cunliffe

Ladybird

Ma famille — My family

Here is a family photograph. Draw your own family photo below and write in French who everyone is.

Maman

Papa

Ma soeur

Mon frère

Dans la maison – In the house

Read the sentences below and find a sticker of each person to put in the room that they like best.

1. **Papa** aime la cuisine.
2. **Maman** aime la salle de bains.
3. **Mon frère** aime le salon.
4. **Ma soeur** aime la chambre.
5. **Grand-père** aime le garage.
6. **Grand-mère** aime le jardin.

Papa   Maman   Mon frère   Ma soeur   Grand-père   Grand-mère

Mes animaux — My animals

Find a sticker for each missing animal and say the animal names in French. Can you find them in the grid below?

chat

poisson

hamster

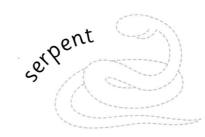
serpent

h	c	h	a	t	p	t	e	r	a
a	y	p	i	o	k	g	m	c	r
m	s	o	u	r	i	s	b	p	a
s	p	i	q	t	u	i	n	c	i
t	x	s	j	u	o	n	a	h	g
e	h	s	f	e	l	a	p	i	n
r	l	o	b	o	o	k	d	e	e
w	j	n	c	f	b	a	v	n	e
o	f	n	g	a	h	n	t	n	r
y	h	s	e	r	p	e	n	t	n

souris

chien

lapin

tortue

araignée

4

Je voudrais – I would like

Choose a sticker pet to go in each pet home. Then complete the sentences.

Je voudrais un poisson.

Je voudrais un _____

_____

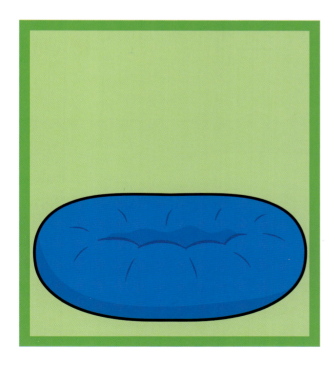

Je _____

_____

Je _____

_____

Les véhicules en ville — Vehicles in town

Say the vehicle names in French and find the missing stickers. Then follow the tracks to take each vehicle home.

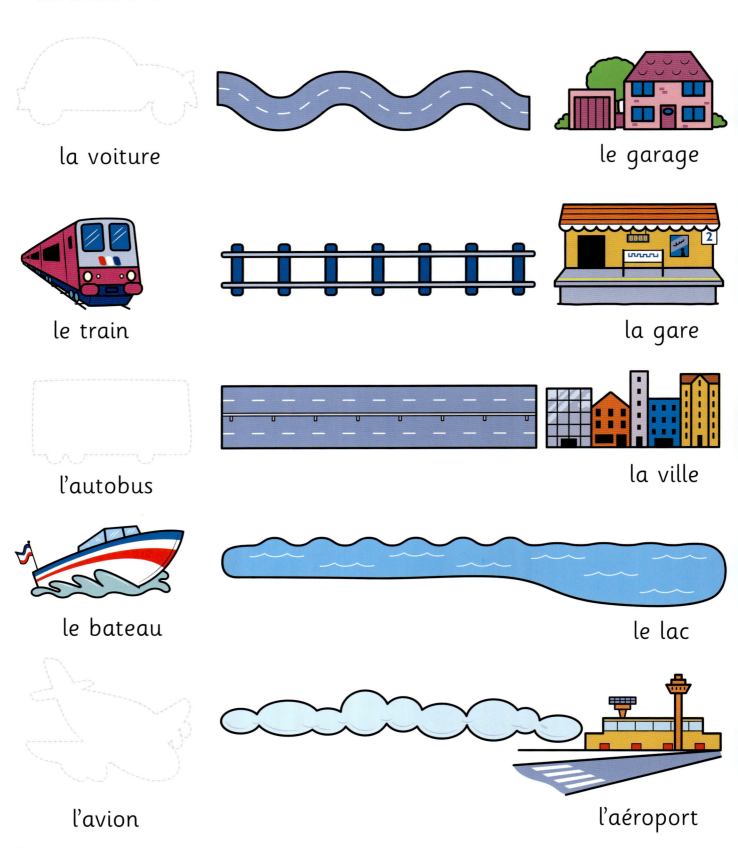

la voiture

le garage

le train

la gare

l'autobus

la ville

le bateau

le lac

l'avion

l'aéroport

Je préfère... — I prefer

Each of these people likes to travel a different way. Find the missing stickers and draw a line from each person to the type of transport that they like best.

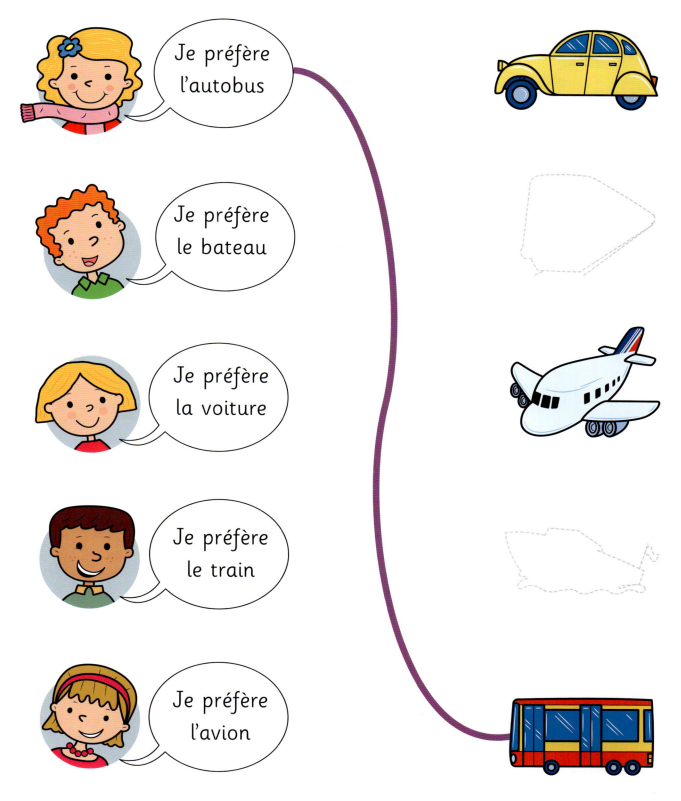

Je préfère l'autobus

Je préfère le bateau

Je préfère la voiture

Je préfère le train

Je préfère l'avion

Les couleurs — Colours

Say the names of the colours in French, then use the key to colour the picture.

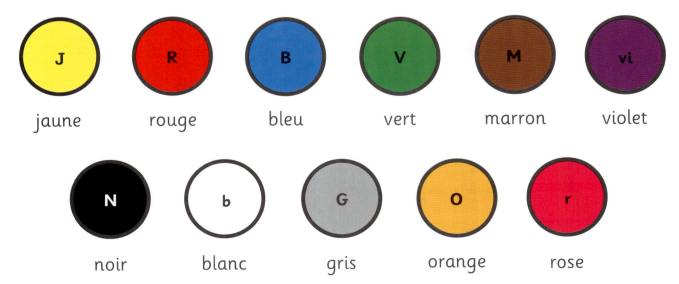

jaune	rouge	bleu	vert	marron	violet

noir	blanc	gris	orange	rose

Les animaux bizarres — Funny animals

Read each sentence and colour each animal that the children can see.

Les nombres à la ferme — Counting at the farm

Say the words in French, and find the missing farm stickers. Write the correct number of things in each box.

un tracteur ☐

deux vaches ☐

trois chevaux ☐

quatre chèvres ☐

cinq cochons ☐

six moutons ☐

sept oies ☐

huit canards ☐

neuf poules ☐

dix escargots ☐

1 un
2 deux
3 trois
4 quatre
5 cinq
6 six
7 sept
8 huit
9 neuf
10 dix

Où habites tu? – Where do you live?

Let's play animal dominoes! Find a sticker home for each animal.

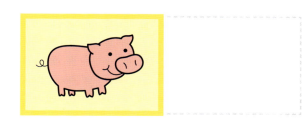

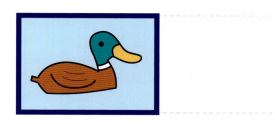

Where do you live?

Où habites tu?   J'habite dans _____

Les contraires – Opposites

Find the missing stickers and join the opposites with a line.

grand

vieil

long

petit

nuit

derrière

devant

jour

jeune

court

Ma famille – page 3

Mes animaux – page 4

Je voudrais – page 5

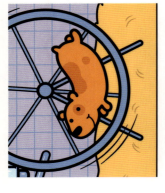   

Les véhicules en ville – page 6

Je préfère... – page 7

Au supermarché – pages 15

C'est petit? C'est grand? – page 16

Bons sons – page 17

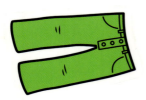 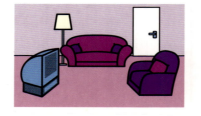 

Au zoo – page 20

Animaux cachés – page 21

un lion	un perroquet	un hippopotame
un tigre	un serpent	des singes

On à quel âge? – page 22

C'est moi – pages 23

Reward – page 24

Les nombres à la ferme – page 10

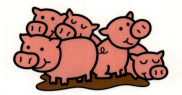
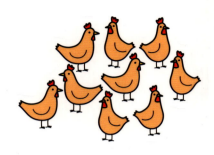
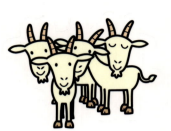

Où habites tu? – page 11

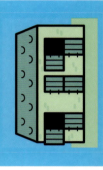

Les contraires – page 12

Using 'un' or 'une' – page 13

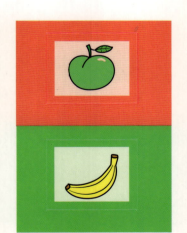

À la fête – page 14

Using 'un' or 'une'

First find the missing stickers then fill in the blanks. If the sentence has **un**, use **petit** or **grand**, if it has **une**, use **petite** or **grande**.

Petit/petite

Voici un petit fromage.

Voici une petite pomme.

Voici une _____ banane.

Voici un _____ pain

Grand/Grande

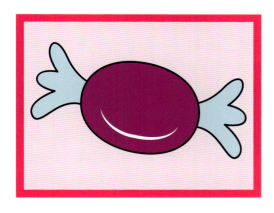

Voici un grand bonbon.

Voici une grande orange.

Voici un _____ fromage.

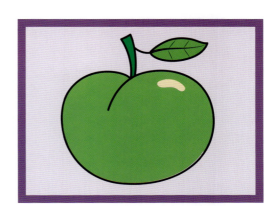

Voici une _____ pomme.

13

À la fête — At the fete

Say each sentence in French. Then find a sticker to give each child what they want.

14

Au supermarché – At the supermarket

Find a sticker of each of the things on the shopping list, and put it in the trolley. Then find a treat and put it in the bag for the way home.

des pommes
des bananes
du fromage
un gâteau
des biscuits
du pain
des oranges
des fraises

15

C'est petit? C'est grand? — Big or small?

Is it big or small? Look at each picture and find the missing stickers.

un ballon
petit

un ballon
grand

une flûte à
bec grande

une flûte à
bec petite

un nounours
petit

un nounours
grand

C'est petit?   C'est grand?

C'est petite?   C'est grande?

Bons sons – Rhyming words

First find the missing stickers, then say the words aloud and join the words that rhyme with a line.

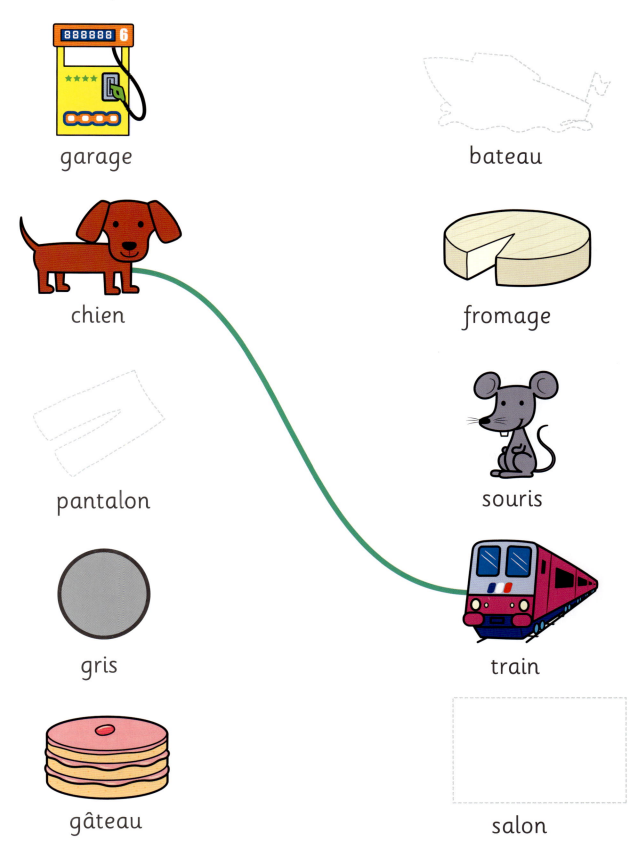

garage

bateau

chien

fromage

pantalon

souris

gris

train

gâteau

salon

Mes jouets – My toys

Read the description and colour each toy.

un nounours rouge

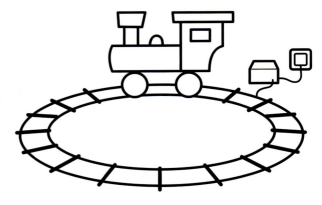

un train électrique marron

une poupée rose

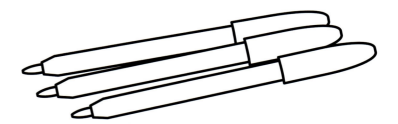

des stylos violets, verts et oranges

un ballon de football
noir et blanc

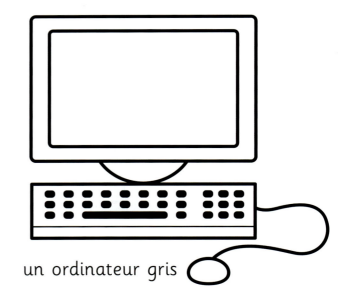

un ordinateur gris

Mes vêtements — My clothes

Say the names of the clothes and colour the picture.

un pull

une écharpe

un chapeau

une casquette

une chemise

des bottes

des chaussures

un t-shirt

une jupe

un pantalon

des baskets

Au zoo – At the zoo

First find the missing stickers, then follow the line from each animal to see where it goes. Which animal is not going back to the zoo?

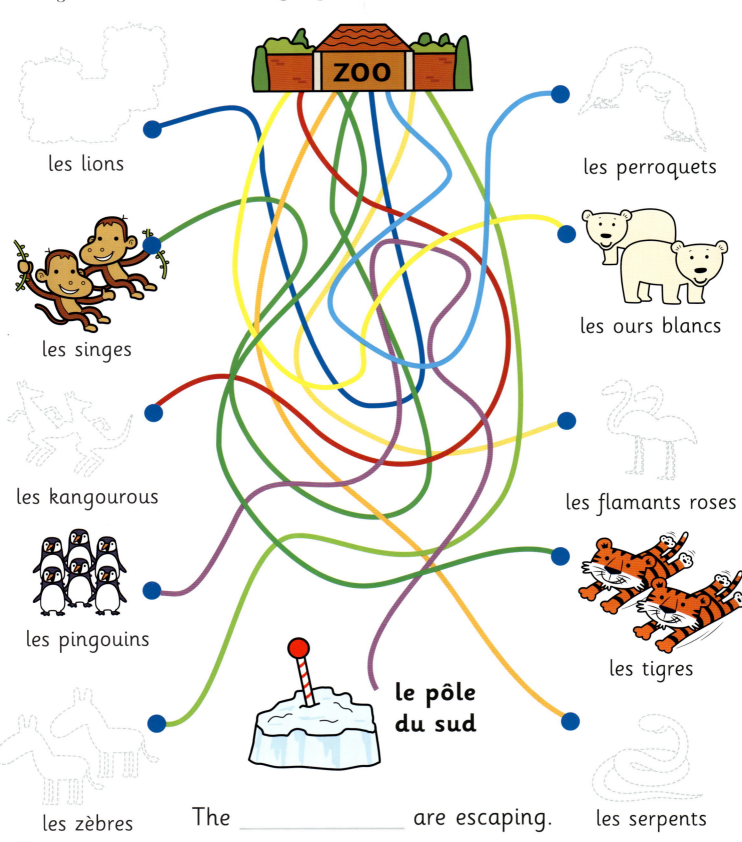

les lions

les perroquets

les singes

les ours blancs

les kangourous

les flamants roses

les pingouins

les tigres

le pôle du sud

ZOO

les zèbres

The _____ are escaping.

les serpents

20

Animaux cachés – Hidden animals

Lots of animals are hiding in this picture. When you spot one, find the matching sticker label and put it by the correct animal.

On a quêl age? – How old are you?

11
onze

12
douze

13
treize

14
quatorze

15
quinze

16
seize

17
dix-sept

18
dix-huit

19
dix-neuf

20
vingt

30
trente

40
quarante

50
cinquante

60
soixante

70
soixante-dix

Say each person's age in French, then mark the missing ages on the picture

- Grand-mère a **60** ans
- Grand-père a **70** ans
- Papa a **40** ans
- Maman a **30** ans
- Mon frère a **12** ans
- Ma soeur a **11** ans

How old are you? Put some sticker candles on this birthday cake.

J'ai _____ ans

22

C'est moi – It's me

Find a picture of Olivier, then draw a picture of yourself and fill in the blanks.

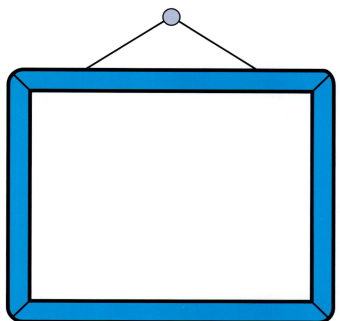

Je m'appelle Olivier.

J'habite à Paris.

J'ai sept ans.

J'aime les vélos.

J'ai un chien.

Je suis petit.

Je m'appelle _____

J'habite _____

J'ai _____ ans.

J'aime les _____

J'ai _____

Je suis _____

Reward chart

Use this chart to keep a record of your progress. Each time you finish an activity, reward yourself with a star. How many can you collect?

I can say these things in French...

- family words
- pets
- I like...
- farm animals
- colours
- types of transport
- how I prefer to travel
- names of different rooms
- numbers to ten
- what I want to eat
- toys
- clothes
- rhyming words
- zoo animals
- opposite words
- 'un' and 'une'
- talk about myself
- say my age